Mycelial Memento Mori

Rebecca Jewell

Presentation by *BookLeaf Publishing*

Web: www.bookleafpub.com

E-mail: info@bookleafpub.com

ISBN: 9789357615495

First edition 2022

*To the starseeds, adventurers, and ones I
love/have loved.*

ACKNOWLEDGEMENT

Thank you to Mama J and Mary Jane for making this collection possible.

PREFACE

Just some things I wrote.

Elegy for Walking

Visit graveyards. Give recitations of
Poems for the dead. Walk softly
Over lichen and moss, then the smallest stones,
Some blank, in the oldest parts of the graveyard,
Like defunct punctuation marks.

Find four stones in a row, each carved with
Only a single word—
MOTHER, FATHER,
GRANDFATHER, JAMES—
These I like best.

Imagine death:
There will be no stones and no
Inscriptions as beautiful as these.
These are for those who are left.

Night Birds Without Wings

The witching hour afoot,
I smoke a cigarette on the wet stoop.
The church bell strikes three.

When I want to destroy things,
you tell me, "No." You say, "Don't burn the
mail,"
Yet you keep nothing for yourself.

I dream about dread, like a mouse among cats,
about hawk feathers in pine needles and how
after dusk they move in the wind, like
us, night birds without wings.

Passersby

Remember the smell of Irish beaches,
store-bought Jaffa cakes in that kitchen,
the coffee never brewed right?
In the driveway, cigarette butts and stones,
colorful things washed ashore and carried there,
the smell of peat moss in the fireplace,
the palm tree in the yard.

Conjure voices of those now silent,
like halos of light while squinting at the
moon—at night
write words to honor the dead
as strange cars pass by; are we just passersby,
who
disappear like wind and burn to black
like busted stars, never uttering "goodbye"?

Speak to the night your dark verses, incantations
that sway like tall grasses, lightly, in the
breeze—
words from lips long closed, recited
from memory, to be heard again in restless
dreams.

I Botched Your Eulogy

Vicodin and baby food make me think of you.

Fuck, you were a strange best
friend/blackout-chef,
Like Emril possessed, making turkey ice cream
sandwiches at 3am. You hiked in pearls, smoked
joints with me
at waterfalls, where we felt at peace.

I bought you Boost for your Chrone's disease,
called you kid,
but all the planning we did about getting old and
still quoting Ron Burgundy in the nursing
home—
I guess it was time wasted really.

I'm sorry I botched your eulogy.

A Crow on Dingle Bay

On the rooftop, a black crow watches
Cameras flash.
The ocean is blue;
The famous Fungi dolphin tour starts soon.
The traveler is nearby with his donkey.

I will see this same crow again, but never know
It is him.
He is, like me, a visible ghost in a tourist trap.

Visiting My Friend after the Death of his Mom

Pushing in chairs around a table might be nothing.
You tidy up the room.
But this time it was more than nothing—the room
still in chaos, walls colored by
panic and fear like shades of slate, like the deep
inhale of shock, like
that stopped moment in time when the lungs will not
release
because maybe, if not, the next terrible moment
won't happen at all.

It is quiet in the house except a ticking, a tapping, of
pacing dog nails
in the upstairs hall. Your voice calls out to no
response.
I think maybe pushing in the chairs is breaking some
unspoken rule,
so I don't want to,
yet I think she would want us to, so we do. We push
in the chairs,
as if that could change things somehow.

Burying Badger (a cat)

She was heavy in my arms.
I was nervous.
My first time dumping a body.

I took her to the woods.
Laid her under ferns.
Said a few words.

The night before I displayed her, wrapped in silks
in a box in the kitchen--
like a nineteenth century Irish wake.

The Burden of Stars

You bear burdens
like the crow perched on that red house in
Ireland:
fearless, facing the sea,
knowing you will survive.

You nourish all things in your presence—
the sunflowers and squirrels, in your charge.

Your light burns steady as an un-flickering star.

Feathers

I watch a hawk in the sky,
remembering the two spotted hawk feathers nestled
among tiny pine cones and pine needles—
near a secret waterfall no one saw but me.

I imagine the Dali tarot card: Death.
I finally understand the darkness where there is room
to let bloom the most exquisite rose—

I finally see in the sky a swallow, feel the lift
of breeze which keeps her afloat, know
there is a rising up, and hope is, like Dickinson wrote,
the feathered thing in the soul
waiting to take flight.

In moonlight, I release it to await its return,
constellations fading to pastels of breaking dawn
against
a melody of bird song.

I go inside and give myself to dreams,
and for the first time find within me a stillness,
like the hushed quiet of the woods,
and think, I must be close to knowing peace.

Breaking Rocks in the Forest
While California Burns

We find primitive campsite #2.
Scouring the rocks, we find a hunk of calcite,
Taking turns
we eagerly smash it against other rocks
to see the crystal structure inside.

On the other side of the country,
California burns;
My brother is there in rivers, mining for gold.

Picking Pinecones in the Apocalyptic Uknown of COVID

You pick pinecones.
Fish swim in cold river water,
air still winter-feeling. Yet, in the sun are
fat robins and brazen chipmunks.
Geese bicker.

The oldest, impossibly tall trees in the forest
churn sunlight to shadow.
In the pine trees, between shafts of light,
an idea stirs:
You are just a visitor in their woods.

The light changes color.
You leave one pinecone behind,
taking only two.
You will keep these on some shelf.
Once in a while, you will glance at them.

Peeling Oranges in Moonlight

Met by dew-covered porch boards,
I am alone, under a sharp-edged moon,
tearing the skin from Valencia oranges
when almost silently, a barefooted man races by
in his boxers, shirtless;
he doesn't notice me watching.

He is running from the pacing shadow-woman
two houses down
whose silhouette moves behind back-lit, foggy
window panes and yellow curtains,
casting shadows on a yard where
on hot afternoons a frowning, smudge-faced girl
stares staring at cars
and kicks muddied stuffed animals into
driveway-pot-holes.

The man has not returned when the stars start
shifting in the dimly-lit, humid sky.

Staring up at the red-tinged light of Mars,
tracking stars and constellations,
I remember the fallen robin's nest,

feeling suddenly in the life-line creases of my
palm
the ghost weight of the dead baby bird I cradled
there.

I toss the orange peels into the grass below
Knowing somewhere nearby, at the edge of tiger
lilies,
among rhubarb and ferns,
a small feathered chest is collapsing in on itself--
soon to be maggot filled.

Before I go, I take in the dark shared between us
Thinking of that woman behind the curtain,
and the smudge-faced girl's troubled dreaming
floating like spider's silk
above her mother's stilted, muted weeping.

Poem Ideas Written in My Notebook

Dragonflies and other bugs I've seen this summer.

Reading Echart Tolle in a recession, after COVID.

The only life event I have on Facebook: I made venison stew in 2019.

Am I too sarcastic to write poetry?

"I'm not really into space": Things real people say.

The Perfect Meal

Burying my Cat

The Dog Needs a Bath Again

These Gel Pens Aren't So Bad

Remember Passing Out

Why I Worship George Saunders

10 Ways to Die as an Adjunct Professor

Floating the River on Mushrooms

You won't regret it--

Even if a fish skips up out of the water
and almost hits you in the face.

Even if there are kids racing on giant inflatable
ducks
yelling about god-knows-what.

The clouds on that sky
mostly looking like turtles and dinosaurs,
like Yoshi from Mario,
they won't disappoint.

That breeze when you hang your head back
the way you'll kick your feet in the water,
even at 6:00pm, even at 36 years old,
will be worth the wet walk home

--floating on mushrooms.

Scarves

The geese on the river make strange ghost calls
in frozen March air. Frost shimmers on stiff
grass,
reflecting the street lights.

I wrap my scarf around my neck, tuck it
into my coat. The scarf is red;
it has me remembering the vole from college.
He was living off of dog food.
He was storing it in closets—in bags of scarves.

For months he hoarded; we were sleeping or
working.
Blind, he made those tunnels into cheap woven
synthetics
Thinking he had saved his life.

My roommate drowned him in a bucket of water.
I was angry about my scarves.

Beware of Dog

You saw me; your gaze
held the power of a thousand upturned faces
smiling at the sky.
Your silence now is the cruelest reprise.

I try burying your words in dirt,
spreading them like ashes, but my lips burn
upon their recitation.
So I whisper instead, an incantation:
Beware of dog.

Acidic Memory

Corrosive, like battery acid:

the feel of your skin, the angles of your teeth,
the expressions you would keep
just for me, to make me laugh.

The memory rancid now

like a carpe corpse with an arrow hole
washed up on the riverbank of the St. Lawrence
stinking of that awful rot

I cannot forget

At Midnight

She reads him Saunders
in dark rooms
They lie together in.

She wants to dismantle him
by the Tenth of December.

Goodbye Summer

sleeping through sunrises
watching constellations chase the moon
wandering forest trails
chasing hawks and ospreys
watching ships head to sea

counting shooting stars
listening to crickets sing along to reggae by a
fire
feeling edges of long grass blades against your
lips
smelling mushrooms in the woods, eyes closed

you will miss this

Foraging for Amanitas

Find them emerging from pine-needle oceans.
Find them near birch, elm, pine, oak that are
broken, lying split open like splintered ships.

Find them reminding you of childhood, of death,
of cosmic nurseries birthing
stars into galactic webs.

(See also, all things impossible: the human
brain,
the whole mycelial network,
a 3D printed lung made possible by Mountain
Dew)

Find in them epiphanous realizations, like sun
peeking through tree veils, ephemeral light
brightening
lichen, moss, slime: How strange is the
persistence of ego
in the face of the sublime.

Cemeteries of the Future

Walking the sand trail as it snakes between
graves, I imagine floating above,
looking down on the honey-comb earth below.

I look at the trinkets gathered around each stone:
broken angel figurines, chunks of polished
quartz,
plastic flower arrangements, a
sardine can, a bottle of aspirin, a hockey puck.

These are the things placed gently
until no one comes to place them anymore.

In future cemeteries, grief too looks like this.

www.ingramcontent.com/pod-product-compliance
Lightning Source LLC
LaVergne TN
LVHW021351200726
843509LV00014B/2785